P9-CMY-768

TEN MONKEY JAMBOREE

by Dianne Ochiltree
pictures by Anne-Sophie Lanquetin

MARGARET K. McELDERRY BOOKS
New York London Toronto Sydney Singapore

TO JIM—LIFE WITH YOU IS A JAMBOREE!

—D. O.

POUR MARITÉ ET PIERRE

—A.-S. L.

Margaret K. McElderry Books
An imprint of Simon & Schuster Children's Publishing
1230 Avenue of the Americas
New York, NY 10020

Book design by Dave Caplan and Sonia Chaghatzbanian
The text of this book is set in Cafeteria.
The illustrations are rendered in inks and pencils.

Printed in Hong Kong
10 9 8 7 6 5 4 3 2 1

Library of Congress Cataloging-in-Publication Data

Ochiltree, Dianne.
Ten monkey jamboree / Dianne Ochiltree ; illustrated by Anne-Sophie Lanquetin.– 1st ed.
p. cm.
Summary: Rhyming text and illustrations demonstrate how many monkeys it takes to make a tail-tangling, tree-dangling jungle jamboree and how many combinations of numbers will add up to ten.

ISBN 0-689-83402-0

[1. Monkeys--Fiction. 2. Addition--Fiction. 3. Counting. 4. Stories in rhyme.] I. Lanquetin, Anne-Sophie, ill. II. Title.
PZ8.3.O25 Te 2001
[E]--dc21
99-089388

One monkey swings in a jungle tree.

"Monkeys, monkeys.

Play with me!

Monkey fun takes more than one.

Won't you join my jamboree?"

Nine monkeys hear him.

They come to play.

One monkey and nine monkeys say,

"Ten monkeys can make a jamboree.

And real monkey fun.

Just watch. You'll see!"

Seven monkeys leap

from tree to tree.

They twist and spin.

Then leap again.

Two monkeys twirl and flip.

Their long tails curl.

They never slip!

One monkey hangs by her knees

in the breeze.

Ten monkeys have a tail-tangling, tree-dangling jungle jamboree.

Two monkeys click sticks.

The music goes ping ping ping!

Four monkeys swing palm leaves that whistle and sing.

Add four more monkeys to keep the beat.

They slap an old log with hands and feet.

Ten monkeys have a music-making,
leaf-shaking
jungle jamboree.

Three monkeys dance on a banana-tree branch.

They flip and flop.

They hop.

Then **PLOP!**

A great big bunch falls off for lunch.

Two monkeys munch mountains of berries.

Five monkeys crunch crispy green leaves.

Ten monkeys have a foot-stomping, snack-chomping jungle jamboree.

Four monkeys see a tiger.

One monkey shouts out, "Run!"

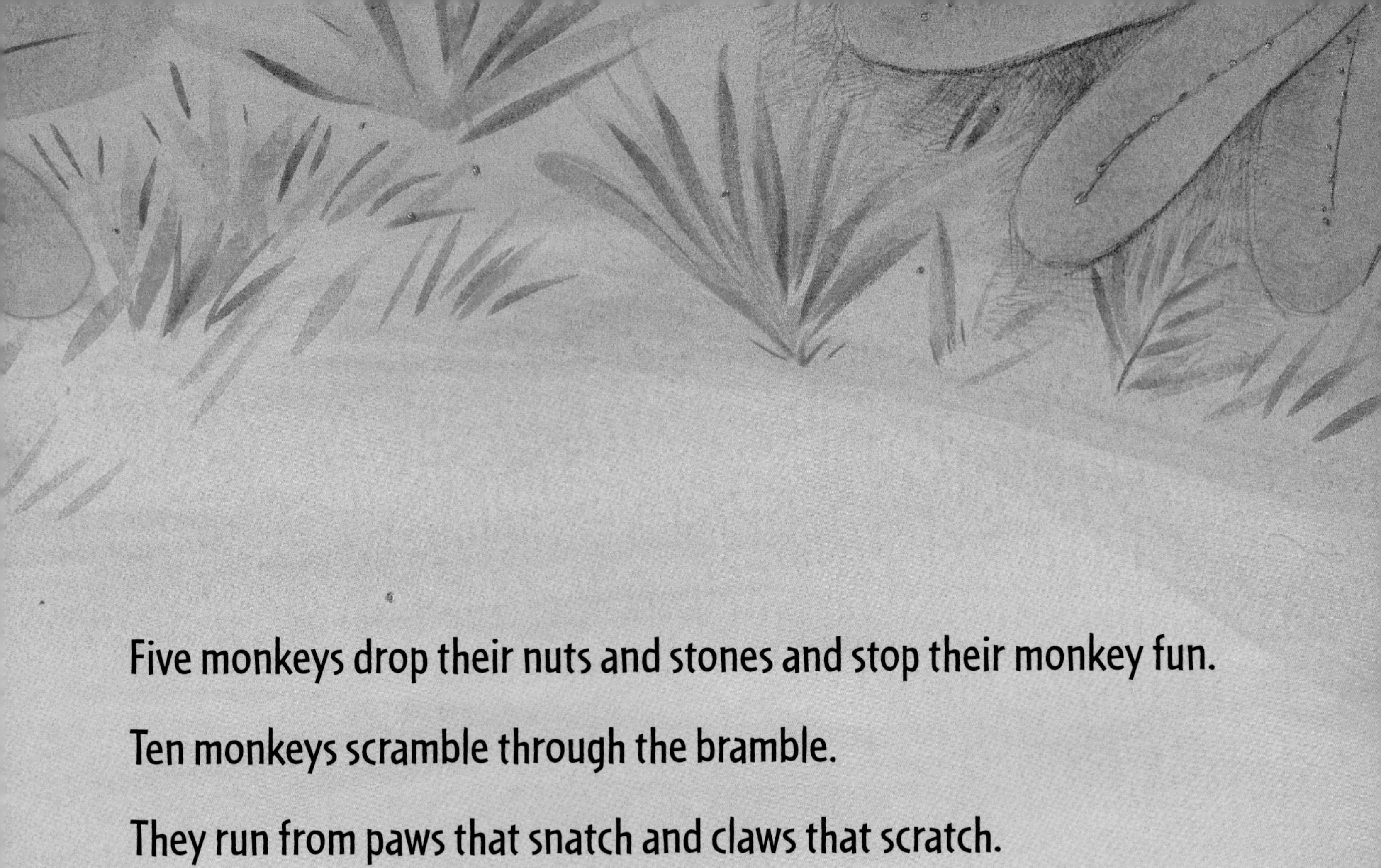

Five monkeys drop their nuts and stones and stop their monkey fun.

Ten monkeys scramble through the bramble.

They run from paws that snatch and claws that scratch.

Ten monkeys have a

tiger-racing, monkey-chasing jungle jamboree.

One by one, they hug the jungle tree.

Now **WHUMP, WHUMP, WHUMP!**

The monkeys jump up.

They climb up high, far from the trap

of tiger jaws that snarl and snap.

Six monkeys screech and show their teeth.

One monkey spits, chatters, and chits.

Three monkeys wave to show they are brave.

Ten monkeys have an **EARSPLITTING,** tree-sitting jungle jamboree.

Then they hide, deep inside clumps of leaves.

They look out over mountains and river and trees.

They keep watch for monkey enemies.

Look closely in the branches.

How many monkeys do you see?

How many monkeys sit and wait

for the next jungle jamboree?